A DINNER DATE WIT

Over dinner, the discussion came round to other sh_____
of new ocean liners. Cunard's *Lusitania* had ente_____
to follow soon afterwards and while White Star had its Big Four, it had no
superliner to compete with the Cunard pair. Lord Pirrie, of Harland & Wolff,
had invited J. Bruce Ismay, the Chairman of the White Star Line, and his wife
to dine at his home, Downshire House, Belgrave Square, London. Both men
drew plans for a trio of superliners, a full third larger than the Cunard liners,
which were then the largest man-made objects in existence. Designed not to
win the Blue Riband, but for comfort and elegance, the ships would have three
funnels and four masts, with the first two being built on the new slipways that
Pirrie was having constructed at his Belfast shipyard. Once one was complete,
its slipway would be used to build the third ship. With three large vessels,
White Star could operate a weekly service from Southampton to New York,
both economically and profitably. The ships were to be the height of luxury,
with every possible convenience on board, including large restaurants, Turkish
Baths and a swimming pool, with a gymnasium, squash courts and an onboard
Post Office, capable of dealing with thousands of items of mail, because the
mail was as important as passengers on the North Atlantic route from Britain
to America.

Titanic leaves
Belfast on 2 April
1912. She would
never return to
the city of her
birth.

Everything about the new ships would be a superlative. They were fully a third larger than *Lusitania* and *Mauretania*, they would have the largest reciprocating engines ever built, they were simply Titanic in size and their names reflected this confidence from their builders. *Olympic* was to be the first ship, her first sister would be *Titanic* and the third vessel was to be *Gigantic*. Each one would be a triumph of the shipbuilder's art and each would, in turn, confirm Harland & Wolff's position as the premier builder of ocean liners in the world. *Olympic* and *Titanic* would be built side by side under the new Arrol Gantry, designed and built by the same firm that had built the Forth Railway Bridge. The Arrol Gantry was 840 feet long, 228 feet high and was 270 feet wide. It was equipped with moving cranes and huge ramps up each side, to be used as the ships were constructed for the steel that would make up the plating on the side of each ship.

The ships themselves would be held together with four million rivets, some hammered in by hand but the majority riveted using state-of-the-art machines. On 16 December, 1908, after much work at the Queens Island yard, the first plates of steel were laid – the ribs of the keel that everything on *Olympic* would branch from. At 882.6 feet in length, with a width of 92.5 feet, *Olympic* would dwarf anything yet built. Barely a decade before a ship of half the size was unimaginable, and here, Harland & Wolff were making a leap into the unknown, building a series of liners, each slightly larger than the last. With a displacement of 60,000 tons and a gross tonnage of 45,324, they were watched with interest by not only other shipping lines and shipyards, but by the general public too. The Press followed the construction with interest and White Star advertised the new ships with gusto. The design was such that leading shipping journals were calling the ships 'practically unsinkable'; a double keel and a series of watertight bulkheads were designed in such a way that five could be damaged and flooded and the ships would still float.

Thomas Andrews

J. Bruce Ismay

On 20 October 1910, the great and the good travelled to Belfast on special trains and chartered steamships for the launch of the first of the trio. Painted in a light grey to aid the throng of photographers who swarmed around the yard and took up position along the banks of the river, all jostling for the best view, the *Olympic* took to the water. Soon, tugs were swarming around her, pulling her to the fitting-out area, where she would be equipped with her boilers, engines and other machinery, and where she would be fitted out, the bare decks being filled with kitchens, storerooms, bedrooms, public rooms and cargo-handling equipment.

Titanic, safely launched,
dwarfs the paddle steamer at
her side on 31 May 1911.

Above: Some of the 15,000
Harland & Wolff employees
who built *Titanic* stand in
front of her older sister.

On the day of the launch of *Olympic*, her sister, *Titanic*, a notice board at her bow proclaiming her name and build number of SS 401, was still part plated but she would soon be ready for launching too. The steelworkers and riveters would be diverted to her, while on board *Olympic*, the carpenters, plumbers, electricians and engineers took over. About six months or so behind *Olympic*, *Titanic* took to the water on 31 May 1910, the same day her sister was handed over to White Star and left Belfast for her first journey to Liverpool and Southampton. That day a record was made; Belfast harbour had over 100,000 tons of shipping in port, 90 per cent of that in two vessels. Many guests had toured *Olympic* in the morning, proclaiming their amazement at the sheer luxury of the new vessel, before viewing the launch of her mighty sister. *Olympic* would have only the second swimming pool ever fitted to an ocean liner, she had electric lifts, the latest in equipment as well as sumptuous suites and Third Class accommodation that was better than many a ship's First Class areas. *Olympic* was a floating wonder and Bruce Ismay proclaimed that her sisters would be even more luxurious.

Olympic left the shipyard on the day *Titanic* was launched.

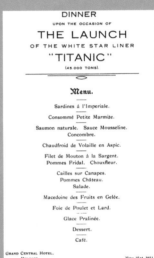

DINNER

UPON THE OCCASION OF

THE LAUNCH

OF THE WHITE STAR LINER

"TITANIC"

(45,000 TONS)

Menu.

Sardines à l'Imperiale.

Consommé Petite Marmite.

Saumon naturale. Sauce Mousseline.
Concombre.

Chaudfroid de Volaille en Aspic.

Filet de Mouton à la Sargent.
Pommes Fridal. Chouxfleur.

Cailles sur Canapes.
Pommes Château.
Salade.

Macedoine des Fruits en Gelée.

Foie de Poulet et Lard.

Glace Pralinée.

Dessert.

Café.

GRAND CENTRAL HOTEL,
BELFAST.   May 31st 1911.

Work began on the interiors of *Titanic*. Some work would be sub-contracted to firms such as Cheltenham's H. H. Martyn, but most of the interior design was completed at Harland & Wolff's huge carpentry works at Belfast and Southampton, the component pieces of each cabin and public area being constructed outside the ship and then marked on the reverse and dismantled for reassembly aboard the ship in Belfast. The huge jigsaw puzzle was coming together, with huge steel castings coming from Darlington, china from Spode and Stonier in the Potteries, the steering equipment from Scotland, massive anchors and chains for each ship also coming from Netherton in the Black Country, while the linen weavers of Northern Ireland produced napkins and table cloths in their thousands for the ships. With 15,000 in the yard alone and a similar number employed indirectly, the ships were a massive undertaking and the pride of all Ireland. All this effort from an after-dinner chat and a few preliminary sketches made that night in London.

Workers leaving Harland & Wolff as *Titanic* is close to being launched in May 1911.

Titanic at Southampton with a dockside crane unloading cargo and supplies into her forward hold.

PRACTICALLY UNSINKABLE

The *Olympic* and *Titanic* were the talk of the world. The publicity machine had been working overtime for months before *Olympic* entered service. She had been branded 'the ship magnificent' and all of the company's brochures, menus for Second and Third Classes and letterheads stated the company was building the 'largest steamers in the world, over 45,000 tons'. Some learned journals had gone as far as to proclaim the ships were 'practically unsinkable'. Postcards were issued of the new liners, cigarette and chocolate tins advertised them; even boxes of matches mentioned the new ships.

The London & South Western Railway, owner of the port of Southampton, had been constructing a new dock for the ships on reclaimed land close to the town's Royal Pier. It was a major undertaking and work had started soon after the announcement that White Star was building the superliners. Work had not been completed before *Olympic*'s maiden arrival in the port on 2 June 1911. In fact, there was much to learn about the handling of such large vessels, as well as the ability of ports to cope with them. White Star were to find out on 20 September 1911 that special care had to be taken with such large ships, especially in the shallow waters of the Solent. Captain E. J. Smith, the most experienced captain in the fleet, and White Star's Senior Captain, took the ship out as normal. When sailing off the Isle of Wight, she steamed close to the cruiser HMS *Hawke*, which was sucked towards the passenger liner. The two ships collided, the armour-piercing bow of *Hawke* making an almost perfect V-shape in the stern of *Olympic*. Neither ship was mortally wounded, but *Hawke*'s bow was stove in and a huge gash in *Olympic*'s side continued far below the waterline. *Hawke* limped off to Portsmouth, while *Olympic* was towed back to Southampton for temporary repairs with wood and concrete before travelling to Belfast to the Thompson Graving Dock, the only dry dock in the world capable of accommodating the ship.

Olympic being rammed by the much smaller HMS *Hawke*. Opposite can be seen the damage to *Olympic* in Southampton's Ocean Dock.

Olympic dressed overall before her maiden voyage in Southampton's Docks.

Olympic in Southampton for the first time, June 1912.

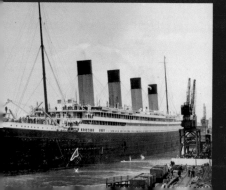

The last rope is cast off as *Titanic* sets sail on her maiden voyage.

Steam up on 1 April 1912. *Titanic*'s sea trials would take place the next day.

Dressed overall, *Titanic* in the Ocean Dock, Southampton, on Good Friday 1910. It would be the only time she was dressed in flags. Coal barges are alongside.

Her repair would take months and some of the thousands of workers swarming over *Titanic* would be sent to work on *Olympic* instead. This was to be the first delay in *Titanic*'s construction. Six weeks after arriving back at Belfast, and at huge cost to White Star, *Olympic* left again to re-enter service. She had proved herself practically unsinkable, for a smaller ship would have been cut in two and lost. In February 1912, *Olympic* would return again to Belfast after losing a propeller blade. *Titanic* was hauled out of dry dock and it would be the last time the ships would be in port together. Both Bruce Ismay and Thomas Andrews, the designer of the ships, had been aboard *Olympic* and had taken copious notes on the workings of the ship and set about to add improvements into the design of *Titanic*. Some of these were done at an early stage but the major external difference between the two ships, the enclosed promenade deck, was not completed until quite late in *Titanic*'s fitting out. It wasn't until late March that the promenade deck was plated over and windows added.

Titanic's maiden voyage, originally scheduled for 20 March, was announced. She would leave Southampton on 10 April 1912, right in the middle of a coal strike in Britain. Leaving Belfast on 2 April, her captain was E. J. Smith, making his last journey before retirement. She sailed directly to Southampton after basic sea trials, and work commenced in equipping her for a life of transatlantic service. Workers still swarmed aboard her, completing a snagging list of work, while stores were loaded onto her – everything from china and silverware to bottled beer, fine wines, and huge quantities of food. Coal was a big problem though and White Star scrambled round, trying to find enough Welsh steam coal to fill the 6,000 tons of bunkers aboard *Titanic*. Other ships' voyages were cancelled so *Titanic* could be coaled and she was opened to the public on Good Friday, with the monies collected going to seamens' charities. Dressed overall in flags, she was a magnificent sight. Behind the scenes, her crew was assembled, and she was readied for her first voyage to New York via Cherbourg and Queenstown. A change of First Officer would be made at Southampton and David Blair would leave, to be replaced by William Murdoch.

Above and Below: *Titanic* outward bound off the Isle of Wight on 10 April 1912. The SY *Alberta* was the King of Belgium's royal yacht and was for sale at the time.

S.S. TITANIC. COWES 10 4 1912

S.Y. Alberta

Queenstown was the last port of call on 11 April 1912. Third Class passengers crowd the aft deck.

On the morning of the tenth, passengers began to arrive at the quay side; some had stayed the night before at the South Western Hotel, from where they could view the ship, while others travelled by special trains from London's Waterloo station. They were shown aboard to their cabins by the stewards and stewardesses, using the new-fangled electric lifts, and began to familiarise themselves with the ship and its myriad corridors and decks. Those in First Class saw the magnificence of the Grand Staircase, with its 'Honour and Glory' clock and glass dome above, while even those in Third Class were greeted by cabins and dormitories greatly superior to anything else afloat. At 12 noon, the last rope was cast off and the ship sailed for Cherbourg, where she would be greeted by the tenders *Nomadic* and *Traffic*, each bringing passengers and mail to the ship. It was dusk as she left and *Titanic*'s portholes were ablaze with light as she sailed into the distance, bound for her last ever sight of land. Queenstown was to be her final port of call and she dropped off some passengers who had taken the short crossing to there, including a Jesuit priest called Father Browne, who had taken many photos of the previous day's voyage, a crew member from Queenstown, who deserted there, plus many sacks of mail, written by the passengers and crew as they made their final farewells to friends and family. In Ireland, another group of emigrants boarded the Irish-built vessel from the passenger tenders *Ireland* and *America*, many not realising they would never reach the New World. 1,385 bags of mail were loaded too. By mid-afternoon, *Titanic* hauled her anchors up and, steam up, she sailed for New York with a complement of 324 First Class, 284 Second Class and 709 Third Class passengers, plus 891 crew.

FIRST CLASS

It was First Class that made *Titanic* special. She had been built with no expense spared for luxury. Her builders had been instructed on a cost plus basis, and the final cost had been $7.5M, or about £2M. A suite aboard cost £870 ($4,350), or about £60,000 in today's money. A much more basic First Class berth was £30 (or about £2,000 today), while a Second Class passage was £12 (or about £800/$1,200) and a Third Class ticket ranged from £3 to £8 (£200 to £500 in today's money). A Third Class ticket price varied depending on the accommodation. For single men, it meant a dormitory; for married families, a cabin.

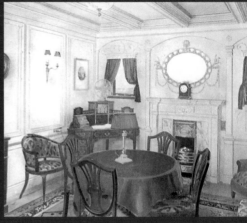

But, back to First Class and its millionaires' suites. First Class on *Titanic* was by far and away the most salubrious on the Atlantic. White Star had given in trying to have the fastest ship on the route, wisely going for luxury and size as the selling points of their vessels. *Titanic* did not disappoint – she was truly the most magnificent of vessels, having only the third swimming pool aboard any ocean liner, a squash court, gymnasium and glamorous public rooms, including a Café Parisien, a la carte restaurant, a sumptuous smoking room and the finest staircase afloat, crowned by a huge glass dome and with a clock surrounded by a carved sculpture of Honour & Glory crowning Time.

Unlike her sister, *Olympic*, *Titanic*'s B Deck had extra cabins added, including two parlour suites, each with its own 50-foot promenade. The First Class Restaurant was enlarged, and, on her starboard side, a Café Parisien was added. The A Deck was fitted with an enclosed promenade area as this area on *Olympic* suffered in bad weather, showering the passengers with sea water and rain in the worst Atlantic storms. The alterations to A and B decks gave *Titanic* a gross tonnage of 46,328 tons, fully 1,004 tons larger than her sister, making her the largest moving object in the world. Much of this size was devoted to First Class accommodations and public areas.

The numerous suites and cabins were finished in a variety of styles from Louis XIV and Adam styles, with many provided with private bathrooms, which were still a novelty on the open sea. First Class was meant to equal the world's best hotels and it did. From the luxurious promenade suites to the smaller cabins for one or two, the ship's accommodation did not disappoint.

SECOND CLASS

Second Class also saw some changes due to the experiences of *Olympic*. Still opulent, certainly in comparison to many other ocean liners, *Titanic* was the pinnacle of Edwardian luxury, with the first electric elevator for Second Class passengers fitted to an ocean-going vessel. Notable Second Class passengers included an English schoolteacher called Lawrence Beesley, who had been photographed by photographers of the *Illustrated London News* on the day of sailing while in the gymnasium. He would go on to write a book about the disaster.

The Second Class accommodations were not as fine as those in First Class but were still luxurious. The dining room was set with long rows of tables rather than the individual tables found in First Class but the Second Class boat deck area was probably the finest on the ship, being located close to the gymnasium. This area would be the scene of high drama as the events of the night of the sinking would unfold.

There were still areas of Second Class unfinished during the maiden voyage and the heating was causing havoc in Second Class. Some cabins were far too hot and others barely above freezing. The novel design of the taps in the bathrooms was also causing issues for some passengers and crew but by the third day of the voyage, those were minor irritations for some. The lift, although a novelty, did ensure that many passengers visited parts of the ship they otherwise would not have. Beesley's comments were that 'whatever else may have been superfluous, lifts certainly were not. Old ladies, for example, in cabins on F deck would hardly have got to the top deck during the whole voyage had they not been able to ring for the lift boy.' He further went on to say that nothing gave a greater impression of the sheer scale of *Titanic* than taking the lift to the various floors and watching the passengers enter and leave the lift.

WHITE STAR LINE.

THE LARGEST STEAMERS IN THE WORLD.

"OLYMPIC" (TRIPLE-SCREW), 45,000 TONS.
AND
"TITANIC" (TRIPLE-SCREW), 45,000 TONS.

Right: A postcard sent off *Titanic* at Queenstown, her last port of call, by Second Class passenger William John 'Jack' Matthews, who was travelling to Chicago from Cornwall. He would never see land again.

The illustrations opposite give an impression of Second Class and show various cabins as well as the Second Class dining room and lounge. A steward serves passengers outside the gymnasium, other passengers promenade and children play next to the lifeboats. On the night of 14/15 April it would all be so different.

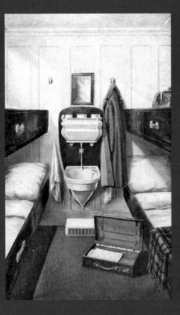

POST CARD

W. H. Stone
Tregonissey
St Austell
Cornwall
England

Dear Bill just a
line to you old boy
just to let you
know I am alright
and well and I
hope you are the
same you can
remember me to
all well good
bye from Jack

THIRD CLASS

The money-maker on any transatlantic ocean liner was not the First Class accommodation but rather the Third Class or Steerage. Emigrants to North America flooded out of Europe, escaping political and religious persecution in Eastern Europe, or just searching for a better life and a new start. From Sweden, Norway, Turkey, France, the United Kingdom and numerous other countries, they made their way to Southampton, Cherbourg and Queenstown (now Cobh) to join the world's largest ship. On some ships, a straw mattress in a dormitory was the height of luxury. For *Titanic* passengers, even those in Third Class, the ship was the ultimate in luxury.

The space that those in Third Class took up represented a small proportion of the passenger space of the ship. Second Class passengers had a huge expanse of the boat deck to use while those in Third Class were kept to the stern of the ship, where they could use the poop deck and the well deck forward of it. The well deck was an area more used to cargo than passengers and large cranes built by Stothert & Pitt in Bath dominated this area. It must not be forgotten that passengers were not *Titanic*'s only cargo. The ship was designed to carry thousands of tons of goods too and on her maiden voyage those included such things as a Renault car and a precious book, studded with precious jewels. *Titanic* had left Southampton with a relatively small Third Class complement but picked up emigrants from many nations in Cherbourg, including Syrians, East Europeans and families from Western Europe too. The two passenger

tenders at Cherbourg were the *Nomadic* and the *Traffic*, which had been built in 1911 and had accompanied *Olympic* from the shipyard. *Nomadic* was intended for First Class passengers while *Traffic*, the smaller ship, was used to take Third Class passengers and luggage to the ships in Cherbourg's outer harbour. *Titanic* would load more human cargo in Queenstown from the tenders *Ireland* and *America*.

Third Class accommodation was spartan, as can be seen from the images below. The cabins had cheap pine walls, instead of the opulent satinwood mahogany, oak amd fine wallpapers of First and Second Classes, while the dining room and other lounges had bare metal walls, painted white. Instead of fine art on the walls, images of the company's fleet sufficed. Food, however, was good, although the choice was much more limited. A typical day's fare would include a choice of oatmeal porridge and milk, boiled Cambridge sausages, Irish stew and bread and butter for breakfast. Dinner would be barley broth, beef a la mode, lima beans and boiled potatoes, with rice pudding or oranges for pudding. Tea would be Leicester brawn, pickles, fresh bread and butter with a compote of apricots and rice and supper would be simply gruel and cheese. According to the menu, issued as a postcard, 'any complaint respecting the food supplied, want of attention or incivility, should be at once reported to the Purser or Chief Purser.'

From *Titanic*'s arrival in Southampton until her departure took a total of eight days. Those days were spent provisioning the ship and preparing her for her maiden voyage. Whole wagon-loads of goods were delivered direct almost to the ship's side, including a prodigious quantity of food, much of which would be consumed on the maiden voyage. Over 6,000 meals were served per day aboard *Titanic*. The table gives an idea of the volume of food consumed aboard on each voyage.

Potatoes 89,600 lb
Fresh Meat 75,000 lb
Poultry and game 25,000 lb
Fresh Fish 11,000 lb
Rice, dried beans, etc.10,000 lb
Sugar 10,000lb
Cereals 10,000 lb
Bacon and ham 7,500 lb
Fresh Butter 6,000 lb
Salt & dried fish 4,000 lb
Onions 3,500 lb
Tomatoes 3,500 lb
Sausages 2,500 lb
Fresh Green Peas 2,500 lb
Coffee 2,200 lb
Ice Cream 1,750 lb
Jams and Marmalade 1,120 lb
Grapes 1,000lb

Tea 800 lb
Fresh Eggs 40,000
Fresh Asparagus 800 bundles
Lettuce 7,000 heads
Sweetbreads 1,000
Flour 250 barrels
Apples 36,000
Oranges 36,000
Lemons 16,000
Grapefruit 13,000
Ales and Stout 15,000 bottles
Minerals 1,200 bottles
Wines 1,000 bottles
Spirits 850 bottles
Fresh Milk 1,500 gallons
Fresh Cream 1,200 quarts
Condensed Milk 600 gallons
Cigars 8,000

As well as food, *Titanic* had to be provisioned with china, silverware, linen and glassware. The china came from various Staffordshire potteries, and the crystal and glassware mainly from Stuart Crystal. Sheffield manufacturers provided much of the silver plate, with Elkington manufacturing thousands of items in its Dubarry pattern for the ship.

In total, there were 57,600 items of china and earthenware, 29,000 pieces of glassware, and 44,000 items of cutlery, each needing stored, ready for use. They were broken down as follows:

Asparagus Tongs 400
Dinner Plates 12,000
Egg Spoons 2,000
Finger Bowls 1,000
Grape Scissors 1,500
Ice Cream Plates 5,500
Nut Crackers 300
Oyster Forks 1,000
Pudding Dishes 1,200
Salt Shakers 2,000
Soufflé Dishes 1,500
Tea Cups 3,000
Wine Glasses 2,000

The linens for *Titanic* were mostly made in Ireland, and included:

Aprons 4,000
Bath Towels 7,500
Bed Covers 3,600
Blankets 7,500
Double Sheets 3,000
Eiderdown Quilts 800
Fine Towels 25,000
Pillow-slips 15,000
Roller Towels 3,500
Single Sheets 15,000
Table Cloths 6,000
Table Napkins 45,000

INFORMATION FOR PASSENGERS.

BREAKFAST at 8 a.m.

LUNCH at 12·30 p.m.   DINNER at 6 p.m

The Bar opens at 8 a.m., and closes at 10·30 p.m.

Lights are extinguished in the Saloon at 11 p.m., and Smoke Room at 12 p.m.

WIRELESS TELEGRAMS.—All Southampton — Cherbourg — Queenstown — New York, Liverpool—Queenstown—New York, Liverpool—Quebec—Montreal, Liverpool—Halifax—Portland, and Liverpool—Queenstown—Boston Mail and Passenger Steamers of the White Star Line are fitted with the Marconi system of Wireless Telegraphy, and messages for despatch should be handed to the Purser.

BAGGAGE.—Questions relating to Baggage should be referred to the Second Steward, who is the Ship's Baggage Master. Trunks, Chairs which Passengers may desire to leave in charge of the Company, should be properly labelled and handed to the Baggage Master on the Wharf at New York, and such articles will be stored entirely at owner's risk. It is necessary for passengers themselves to see all their Baggage is passed by the U.S. Customs Authorities on landing.

PASSENGERS are requested to ask for a Receipt on the Company's Form, for any additional Passage Money, Chair Hire, or Freight paid on board.

SMOKING is strictly prohibited in any of the Staterooms, Library or Dining Saloon.

LIBRARY. Books can be obtained on applying to the Library Steward.

POSTAGE STAMPS can be obtained from the Saloon Steward, in the Dining Saloon who will take charge of Cable Despatches and Telegrams for transmission from Cherbourg and Queenstown. Such Cable Despatches and Telegrams should be handed to the Saloon Steward an hour before arrival at these ports.

MEALS not permitted to be served in the Library.

SECOND CLASS PASSENGERS are not allowed on the First or Third Class Decks.

DECK CHAIRS can be hired at a charge of 4/- each for the voyage.

STEAMER RUGS can be hired at a charge of 4/- for the voyage.

VALUABLES.—The White Star Line has provided a safe in the office of the Purser in which Passengers may deposit money, jewels, or ornaments for safe keeping. The Company will not be liable to Passengers for the loss of money, jewels, or ornaments by theft or otherwise, not so deposited.

THE SURGEON is authorised to make customary charges, subject in each case to the approval of the Commander, for treating Passengers at their request for any illness not originating on board the ship. In the case of sickness developed on board, no charge will be made, and medicine will be provided free in all circumstances.

The Purser is prepared for the convenience of Passengers to exchange a limited amount of English and American money, and he will allow at the rate of $4.80 to the £1 when giving American money for English currency, or £1 to $4.95 when giving English for American money.

The following rates of exchange have also been adopted for American and French money—Eastbound $1 = 5 francs; Westbound, Notes and Gold = 19 cents per franc, Silver = 18 cents per franc.

TRAVELLERS' CHEQUES, payable in all parts of Europe, can be purchased at all the principal offices of the White Star Line. These Cheques are accepted on board White Star steamers in payment of accounts, but the Pursers do not carry funds to enable them to cash same.

PASSENGERS' ADDRESSES may be left with the Saloon Steward, in order that any letters sent to the care of the Company may be forwarded.

DOGS. Passengers are notified that dogs cannot be landed in Great Britain, unless a license has previously been procured from the Board of Agriculture, London. Forms of license must be obtained by direct application to the Department before the dog is taken on board

MAIDEN VOYAGE

Towering above the Southampton skyline, as her sister had done proudly ten months before, *Titanic* was prepared for her maiden voyage. Work was still continuing aboard, and fresh flowers had been placed everywhere to mask the smells of paint that still permeated the ship. All around was a hive of activity as crew members rushed around in preparation for the throng that would descend on the ship through the course of the morning. Those crew not needed before today rushed to the ship before crew muster and stowed their bags away and got to work. The boilers were already being stoked and Thomas Andrews had boarded at 6 a.m. Many passengers had stayed over in the luxurious South Western Hotel, others in boarding houses around the dock area, but many were also coming from London in the two special boat trains that would leave Waterloo.

By twelve, the ship was ready and the ropes were let go. Crowds thronged the pier to say goodbye to loved ones as passengers swarmed on deck to wave England goodbye, many who were emigrating for what would have been their last time. Already the ship was a veritable melting pot of cultures from Americans and British people to Scandinavians and the French.

At twelve, *Titanic* left berth 44. Tugs hauled her from the dockside and she nudged her way into the river Test. Because of the coal strike that had just finished many steamers were berthed up and *Titanic* had to steam past the SS *New York*, an American Line ship, berthed next to the White Star's own *Oceanic* at berth 38. As *Titanic* put on speed she came level to the *New York* and literally sucked her away from the side of *Oceanic*. *New York*'s mooring ropes snapped as if they were twine and only the quick thinking of the tug captains, especially of the *Vulcan*, saw disaster averted. The *New York* was nudged away from the *Titanic* just in time. *Titanic* was delayed as the *New York* was made secure. Soon she was on her way to Cherbourg and lunch was served, passengers being called by a bugler playing 'The Roast Beef of Old England'.

Loading passengers and mail in Cherbourg at dusk, the lights of *Titanic* blazed and she made a fine sight in the outer harbour. Soon she would set sail for Queenstown, where she would arrive on Thursday morning. Passengers disembarked at Queentown, including a Jesuit priest, Father Browne, whose photographs of his voyage would leave an enduring record of the short life of this magnificent ship. As well as people leaving, and mail being delivered to the ship's post office (over 1,300 sacks), passengers furiously completed final letters home. Most mail from Queenstown was stamped with a 3.45 p.m. Queenstown postmark, but some carried the ship's own special transatlantic post office postmark too.

The passengers soon settled into a routine of shipboard life. Those in First Class spent time in the palatial public rooms and in their large cabins. Some

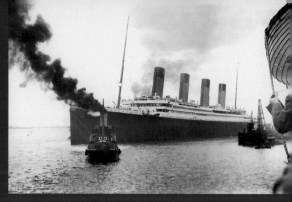

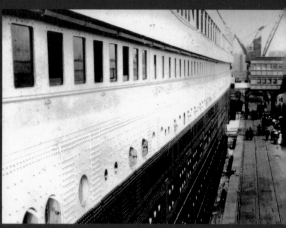

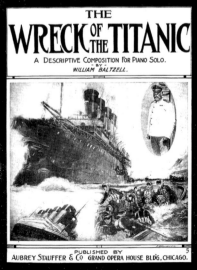

IN MEMORIAM

TO THE
BRAVE MUSICIANS
WHO PLAYED THE
LAST REQUIEM
FOR THE PASSENGERS
OF THE
TITANIC.

THE
WRECK OF THE TITANIC
A DESCRIPTIVE COMPOSITION FOR PIANO SOLO.
BY
WILLIAM BALTZELL.

PUBLISHED BY
AUBREY STAUFFER & CO GRAND OPERA HOUSE BLDG, CHICAGO.
5

ON SALE AT FINE MUSIC STORES

All Proceeds From The Sale of The Wreck of The TITANIC Will be
Distributed Among The Grieving Families of The Musicians Who Died
Aboard The Ill-fated Liner

(347)

promenaded and others preferred the pleasure of their own private verandahs. In Third Class, music from Irish pipes and violins could be heard. Some passengers read, others gossiped but all were impressed with this new queen of the sea.

The voyage, after the excitement of the *New York* incident, was passing quietly and quickly. It would all change dramatically on Sunday night. Warnings of ice had been coming in all day. The radio operators, Harold Bride and Jack Phillips, were receiving warnings as they also sent passengers' telegrams to friends ashore. Despite the warnings, extra boilers were being brought into service and speed was increasing. Sunday religious services had been performed, dinner had been served and passengers were relaxing or in bed when the inevitable happened and the ship, despite being in open ocean, hundreds of miles from land, steamed into a huge iceberg, puncturing her side. The Captain was soon woken and the ship inspected. Soon, it was obvious she was doomed and Captain Smith ordered an SOS to be broadcast and the ship's boats prepared for launching. Few passengers believed that the ship, that 'as far as it is possible to do so ... is designed to be unsinkable', was actually doomed but she was. Within three hours, the then-largest ship in the world would be gone, broken in two, with over 1,500 of her passengers and crew dead.

Many tales of heroism could be related of that fateful night, as well as tales of cowardice, but the characters that deserve special mention include the engineers who kept the ship's power going to the last, and who all died, the musicians who played almost to the end and the wireless operators who stayed at their posts till the batteries failed. As the final boats left the ship, it was obvious to those left that she was doomed. For one man, alone in front of the fire of the smoking room, a dream had died. Thomas Andrews, one of the visionaries who had created this magnificent ship, died aboard her a broken man.

The thirteen recovered lifeboats in New York. They were soon picked clean of souvenirs of the sinking.

THE LIFEBOATS

Twenty lifeboats with a capacity of 1,178 persons were onboard the *Titanic*. Over 2,200 people were on the sinking ship and only 705 were rescued.

Much has been written about the *Titanic* disaster in the 100 years since the sinking and reference is being made even today whenever a shipwreck occurs, such as that of *Costa Concordia*. The main difference between modern shipwrecks and that of the *Titanic* is that a modern ship carries more than enough lifeboats to rescue every soul on board. It was one of the most far-reaching results of the disaster – lifeboats for all.

Titanic had lifeboat capacity for 52 per cent of those aboard, and less than 50 per cent capacity if the ship was travelling full. This stemmed from a Board of Trade regulation that stated that ships over 10,000 tons must carry a minimum of sixteen lifeboats. These regulations were woefully out of date and, even at the time of disaster, moves were afoot to change the regulations although no decision had been made.

Alexander Carlisle, one of the driving forces of Harland & Wolff, had left the company to work with the Welin Davit Co. and so Harland & Wolff were no strangers to the regulations concerning lifeboats. Despite the lack of lifeboat capacity, *Titanic* was within the law. A new davit type had been considered for the ship – one which would cope with 48 lifeboats – but it was decided to have only 20 lifeboats fitted, four above the legal minimum. This decision was to

cost 1,500 lives. There is no doubt that had there been more lifeboats almost all aboard the ship would have been rescued. The sea was calm, the ship sank on an even keel and it took over two hours for her to go down. Of course, *Titanic* was 'practically unsinkable', and this fallacy led to the lack of lifeboat provision.

The majority of the lifeboats themselves were constructed to a Board of Trade-approved design and had been designed by the chief draughtsman, Roderick Robert Crispin Chisholm, who was lost in the disaster as one of the nine-man Guarantee Group from Harland & Wolff. The lifeboats were of three different designs, with the majority being clinker-built wooden lifeboats, of 30ft in length by 9ft 1in breadth and 4ft in depth from keel to rowlocks. These fourteen lifeboats were numbered evenly on the port side and odd numbers on starboard. They were grouped in two sets on each side. With elm keels and evenly spaced elm timbers, the stern and stem posts were built of oak and the boats clad in yellow pine, double fastened with copper nails (so as they would not rust) then painted white. Each had copper buoyancy tanks and the seats were made of pitch pine. Around the gunwales were lifelines.

The ship itself was fitted with Welin davits of a new type, capable of launching three times, and the davit blocks were made of elm with lignum vitae roller sheaves, trebled for the ordinary lifeboats but just doubled for the smaller and lighter emergency cutters. Each lifeboat was equipped with a water beaker and provision tank and a sail, stored in a painted canvas bag, as well as all of the requisites demanded by the Board of Trade. These included blankets, provisions and flares, as well as a spirit boat compass and fitting, the compasses being stowed in lockers on the boat deck. Obviously, one of the things done before the lifeboat was launched was to fill the water tank and provision the lifeboat. Each of the 14 lifeboats was capable of carrying 65 people and could be lowered from the boat deck full to capacity.

Two emergency cutters were fitted forward of the main lifeboats. These were always swung-out, ready for use at any time, and were meant to be used if someone fell overboard or a boat was needed to be sent off to another ship.

With a capacity of just forty persons, the emergency cutters were smaller than the standard lifeboats, with dimensions of 25ft 2in by 7ft 2in. Each was provisioned and supplied with a mast and sail. No.1 was located on the starboard side and No.2 on the port.

As well as these lifeboats, *Titanic* was fitted with four boats of an Engelhardt design. Captain Engelhardt, a Dane, designed the collapsible lifeboat at the turn of the twentieth century. It was designed to work as a raft, or, with its canvas sides up, as a lifeboat. In calm seas, it would float, laden with 4,000kg, or the weight of forty people, with a 3–4 inch freeboard. Each was constructed of wood, with kapok (a kind of cork) as a buoyancy aid. The ones on *Titanic* had a capacity of 47 persons and were 27ft 5in long by 8ft breadth and 3ft in height. Stowed upside down, they were intended to be launched from davits after the wooden lifeboats had been launched. They could be stored flat on the deck or against a bulkhead, thereby using relatively little deck space, which was the issue with the number of lifeboats on the boat deck and why their numbers had been cut from 48, to 32 and then the paltry 16 onboard when the ship sailed. Two of the Engelhardts were stowed on the roof of the officers' quarters, either side of the forward funnel, and two stowed beside the emergency cutters.

The Engelhardts were robust, and three survived in the water to be rediscovered. Collapsible B was sunk with axes during the recovery of bodies, Collapsible A was found floating with three bodies in it a full month after the disaster by the *Oceanic*, while one boat, possibly Collapsible C, was discovered nearly eighteen months afterwards, having floated for 1,800 miles almost to the entrance to the Caribbean. It was brought back to Avonmouth onboard an Elders & Fyffes ship.

Thirteen lifeboats were recovered by the *Carpathia* and taken to New York, where they lay for a while, having been robbed of many items, including oars, nameplates and lifebelts left aboard. Seven were cast adrift, including all four collapsible boats and three ordinary lifeboats. Four lifeboats were never seen again.

One of the failings of the officers on board the *Titanic* was not ensuring all of the boats left full. If they had, another 473 people would have been saved, total capacity being 1,178 persons, against 705 saved. This would have ensured every woman and child plus many men would have lived to tell their story. Some were sent down the falls part full as there were not enough people who were either in the vicinity or who would go in a lifeboat as they began to be launched. Those that opted to stay obviously decided the ship was not going to sink. Many boats were also launched partially full because the officers did not think they could be launched fully laden. All in all, it was a poor showing, and one that could have been resolved by ensuring the boats came back to the ship to be fully laden at a later point.

The disaster focused the mind of the Board of Trade and immediately after the sinking a huge number of lifeboats were constructed to fit aboard ocean liners. Nowadays, every ship carries enough lifeboats and life rafts for all crew and passengers, although the *Costa Concordia* sinking demonstrates clearly that there needs to be enough capacity, even if lifeboats on one side are unusable due to listing.

Lifeboat launching sequence
23.40: *Titanic* collides with iceberg
12.20: Lifeboats swung out
12.30: Women and children begin to be placed in lifeboats
12.45: Lifeboat No.7 launched
12.55: Lifeboat No.5 launched
12.55: Lifeboat No.6 launched
01.00: Lifeboat No.3 launched
01.00: Lifeboat No.1 launched
01.10: Lifeboat No.8 launched
01.20: Lifeboat No.10 launched
01.20: Lifeboat No.9 launched
01.25: Lifeboat No.12 launched
01.30: Lifeboat No.14 launched
01.30: Lifeboat No.13 launched

The ice floe as seen on the morning of 15 April, from a nearby ship. Emigrants look out into the ice pack.

The first boats leave *Titanic*. The boat deck was 75ft above sea level.

↓ 75 FEET FROM BOAT DECK TO WATER.

Awaiting news outside the White Star offices in New York.

01.35: Lifeboat No.16 launched
01.35: Lifeboat No.15 launched
01.40: Collapsible C launched
01.45: Lifeboat No.2 launched
01.45: Lifeboat No.11 launched
01.55: Lifeboat No.4 launched
02.05: Collapsible D launched
02.20: Collapsible A floats off
02.20: Collapsible B washes off deck upside down
02.20 *Titanic* sinks

Top: Some of the crew of the *Carpathia* involved in the rescue of the *Titanic* survivors. On the left are the stewards and on the right are the doctor and some of the female nurses. The first lifeboats approached *Carpathia* in the dark but the last was not recoverd till 8 a.m. In all, barely 700 of the passengers and crew were rescued out of 2,200 aboard.

Titanic makes her final journey, 14,000ft to the ocean floor.